The ETF Advantage

Leveraging Exchange-Traded Funds for Portfolio Diversification

Robert M. Watson

Disclaimer

The information provided in this book is for general informational purposes only and is not intended to be, and should not be taken as, financial, investment, or legal advice. The author and publisher of this book are not financial advisors and do not endorse or recommend any particular investment or financial strategy.

Investing involves risk, including the risk of loss. The value of your investments may fluctuate and you may lose money. Past performance is not indicative of future results. It is important to carefully consider your financial goals, risk tolerance, and other personal factors before making any investment decisions.

You should consult with a financial professional before making any investment decisions and carefully review all relevant documents, including prospectuses, before investing. The author and publisher of this book are not responsible for any errors or omissions, or for any actions taken based on the information contained in this book.

This book is not a substitute for professional financial advice and should not be relied upon as such. The author and publisher of this book do not guarantee the accuracy, completeness, or usefulness of the information contained in this book and will not be liable for any errors or omissions, or for any actions taken based on the information contained in this book.

This book was created with the assistance of an artificial intelligence writing tool. Certain portions of the content were either initially drafted or edited with its help.

4

Contents

Chapter 1: Understanding the Basics of Exchange-Traded Funds (ETFs)

1.1 Defining ETFs

Imagine you were at an all-you-can-eat buffet, but instead of filling your plate with just one item, like pasta, you were able to scoop up a little bit of everything. Now imagine if you could do the same with your investment portfolio— sounds pretty neat, right? Well, that's the concept behind Exchange-Traded Funds or ETFs.

ETFs are an assortment of securities that are traded, much like individual stocks, on an exchange. These securities can include stocks, bonds, commodities, or a mix of investment types. That's right, it's like an investment smorgasbord right on your plate.

But, ETFs are more than just a convenient financial platter. They are designed to track a specific index such as the S&P 500, but they can also track a sector, commodity, or a range of other assets. Their goal is to provide investors with a benchmark return at a minimal cost, while allowing them to stay fully invested and maintain asset allocation.

Now, you might be thinking, "Wait, isn't that the same as a mutual fund?" Well, astute reader, while there are similarities, ETFs differ from mutual funds in some important ways. Unlike mutual funds, ETF shares are traded on a national stock exchange and at market prices that may or may not be the same as the net asset value (NAV) of the shares. This means you can buy and sell them throughout the trading day, just like your favorite tech stock or that disappointing airline share.

To put it plainly, think of an ETF as a basket of assets that you can buy or sell through a brokerage firm on a stock exchange. This ETF basket is designed to track the performance of a specific index or sector. The idea is that you're not putting all your eggs (investments) in one basket (a single stock). Instead, you are spreading them out across a bigger basket, thereby diversifying your holdings.

And in case you're still scratching your head about all this, don't worry. We're just getting started. There's plenty more where this came from. Just remember: an ETF is not a type of equity but a vehicle that tracks various asset classes. It's like taking a bus tour to see a city rather than walking to each site—you get to see it all, and it's much less leg work.

1.2 The History and Evolution of ETFs

A trip down the financial memory lane will lead us to the birthplace of ETFs. It was the early 1990s, a time when neon colors were in, the internet was dial-up, and Nirvana was on the radio. Amidst this setting, the first ETF made its grand entrance into the world of finance.

This prodigious financial innovation was born in the United States, debuting on the American Stock Exchange (AMEX) in 1993. Known as SPDR (pronounced 'spider'), the Standard & Poor's Depositary Receipt, this baby ETF was designed to track the S&P 500 index. For the first time, investors could now trade a single security that provides the investment performance of an entire index. You could call it a 'one-stop shop' for index investing, minus the leg warmers and scrunchies of course.

ETFs initially gained attention for their tax efficiency and lower costs compared to traditional mutual funds, making them quite the Wall Street heartthrob. Over the years, as investors started seeing the value in indexing and the benefits of ETFs, they began pouring money into them. And as they say, money talks.

From their humble beginnings in the early 90s, ETFs have expanded in number, types, and strategies. Today, you have ETFs that track almost every conceivable segment of the market, from broad indices to specific sectors, from bonds to commodities, from regional to global markets, and even niche areas like cybersecurity and clean energy. It's like having a world of investment opportunities right at your fingertips, or should we say, mouse clicks.

But wait, the evolution didn't stop there. Enter thematic ETFs, smart beta ETFs, actively managed ETFs, and the more recent entrants to the ETF landscape - the ESG and cryptocurrency ETFs. But we're getting ahead of ourselves. We'll unpack these in later chapters, so hold on to your financial hats.

In a nutshell, the history of ETFs is a tale of innovation and growth, a financial "from rags to riches" story, minus the rags, but with plenty of figures. Today, the ETF market has exploded into trillions of dollars globally, making it one of the most significant phenomena in finance over the past few decades. And to think, it all started with a simple desire to diversify and simplify investing.

1.3 Types of ETFs

Pop quiz time! What do pizza, ice cream, and ETFs have in common? Answer: endless varieties! From pineapple and pepperoni pizza to mint chip and rocky road ice cream, the choices are abundant and appetizing. Similarly, the ETF universe is abundant and appetizing for investors, albeit less delicious.

Let's start with the basic distinction: Index ETFs and Active ETFs. Index ETFs are the most common type and aim to replicate the performance of a specific index like the S&P 500. They are passively managed, which in finance-speak means they just follow the lead of an index rather than trying to outperform it. Think of them like a mirror reflecting the market – what you see is what you get.

On the other hand, Active ETFs are managed by folks who actively try to beat the market, instead of just mirroring it. They pick and choose their investments, which sounds fun, but picking stocks is not the same as picking your dinner from a menu. But more on that in Chapter 5.

Next, let's dive into the wide array of specific types of ETFs:

Equity ETFs: These are the most common type, investing in stocks of individual companies. Imagine having a piece of all the top companies in the U.S without having to buy each stock individually. Pretty neat, huh?

Bond ETFs: For those who prefer a less rollercoaster-like investing experience, these ETFs invest in bonds, providing regular income and lower risk compared to equity ETFs. It's like choosing the scenic, calm route instead of the adrenaline-inducing rollercoaster ride.

Sector and Industry ETFs: Want to invest in a specific sector like technology or consumer goods? There's an ETF for that. These let you invest in a particular industry without the risk of investing in individual companies. It's like supporting all teams in a league instead of betting on one.

Commodity ETFs: Fancy a gold rush? Or perhaps an oil adventure? Commodity ETFs have got you covered. These invest in physical commodities like precious metals, oil, or agricultural goods. But be warned, these ETFs aren't for the faint-hearted!

International and Global ETFs: Want to add some international flair to your portfolio? These ETFs invest in foreign markets, giving you exposure to the global economy. It's like taking a world tour without leaving your comfy couch.

Currency ETFs: If playing with money is your thing, Currency ETFs let you invest in foreign currencies like the Euro, the Yen, or the Pound. Though, currency markets can be as unpredictable as the British weather.

Inverse and Leveraged ETFs: Feeling adventurous? These exotic-sounding ETFs allow you to profit from market declines or multiply your exposure to an index. But tread carefully, these are complex financial instruments and not suitable for beginners.

Thematic and ESG ETFs: Want to invest in the future or align investments with your values? These ETFs focus on emerging trends like artificial intelligence or environmental, social, and governance (ESG) criteria.

With such an extensive menu, it might seem overwhelming, but don't worry. The right choice depends on your individual needs, financial goals, and risk tolerance. The ETF world is your oyster, so feel free to explore! But don't forget to keep an eye on the price (expense ratio), no one likes an overpriced meal, right?

1.4 Benefits and Risks of ETF Investing

Buckle up, folks, it's time to weigh the pros and cons of our financial vehicle - the ETFs. Every investment vehicle comes with its own GPS system guiding you to the land of profits, but also has potential pitfalls on the route.

Let's start with the shiny side, the benefits of ETFs:

Diversification: Imagine putting all your money on one horse in a race. Now imagine spreading your bet across all horses. Which seems safer? ETFs offer instant diversification as they consist of many different assets. It's like investing in the entire horse race, not just one stallion.

Flexibility: ETFs are traded like stocks, which means you can buy and sell them throughout the trading day at fluctuating prices. If you're the kind of person who can't wait for the market to close, ETFs have you covered.

Access to Various Markets: Fancy international stocks? Or maybe commodities like gold? ETFs provide access to various markets, sectors, and asset classes which may be difficult to reach otherwise. It's like having a VIP pass to all the financial markets.

Lower Costs: Generally, ETFs have lower expense ratios compared to mutual funds. This is because most ETFs are passively managed and aim to replicate an index rather than beat the market. You see, in the world of finance, less meddling often means less spending.

Transparency: ETFs disclose their holdings daily, so you always know what's inside your investment vehicle. It's like having a clear suitcase - no hidden baggage here!

Sounds like a pretty sweet deal, right? But hold your horses, let's not get carried away. It's important to understand that every silver lining has a cloud. Here are some risks associated with ETFs:

Market Risk: Just like with any investment, you are exposed to the ups and downs of the market. When the assets the ETF tracks decrease in value, the ETF decreases in value too. In other words, when the horses fall, so do your bets.

Liquidity Risk: Some ETFs track obscure or less popular indices. These might be harder to sell during market downturns. If the party gets wild, these ETFs could be left without a dance partner.

Tracking Error: Sometimes, an ETF doesn't do a great job of following its index due to fees or other factors. This discrepancy is known as tracking error. When you're mirroring dance moves, you don't want to miss a step, right?

Leveraged and Inverse ETF Risks: Remember the adventurous-sounding ETFs we talked about? While they promise higher returns or profits from market declines, they also come with greater risk and can lead to significant losses. It's like dancing on a tightrope - thrilling but risky.

There you have it - a balanced view of ETFs. They offer a whole lot of advantages but come with their own set of risks. Understanding both sides of the coin can help you make informed investment decisions. It's all about the balance, after all, we're trying to make money, not ride a rollercoaster. Or were we?

Chapter 2: Diversification 101

2.1 Understanding Diversification

Welcome to Diversification 101, where we'll peel back the layers of this investment strategy faster than you can say, "I love compound interest." We promise this class will be more fun than your high school calculus class, and probably more beneficial, too. Let's dive right in!

Diversification, in the context of investing, is all about spreading your eggs across different baskets, or more accurately, spreading your dollars across different investments. It's the financial equivalent of not betting all your money on the underdog in a race just because your gut tells you to. Instead, you prudently spread your bets across multiple runners, enhancing your chances of success.

Think of it this way: imagine planning a road trip. You wouldn't rely on a single map, would you? In today's world, you would probably use a GPS, a physical map, road signs, and maybe even the stars if you're feeling particularly adventurous. This is diversification at work.

When it comes to investing, diversification might involve spreading your investments across different asset classes such as stocks, bonds, and cash, or across different sectors like technology, healthcare, or utilities. But that's not all; you can also diversify geographically by investing in both domestic and international markets.

Why bother with all this? Well, the rationale is quite simple: not all investments perform well at the same time.

When one investment or sector is down, another might be up, smoothing out the potential bumps in your investment journey. In essence, diversification can help reduce risk and potentially enhance returns over time. And let's face it, who wouldn't like a smoother ride and potentially more cash in their pockets?

Though, while diversification can help manage risk, it doesn't entirely eliminate it. Before you start diversifying like there's no tomorrow, it's essential to understand that every investment comes with some level of risk. But hey, no pain, no gain, right?

2.2 The Role of Diversification in Investing

Now that you're in on the secret sauce of investing, let's explore why diversification plays such a starring role. Consider this: when you plan a party, would you only serve one type of food or play one genre of music? Probably not, because you know that variety is the spice of life. The same principle applies to your investment portfolio.

Diversification plays the role of a risk manager for your investments. Picture this: you're on a boat, and that boat is your portfolio. Diversification is the person distributing the weight evenly across the boat to keep it stable. By spreading investments across various asset classes, sectors, and geographic regions, you're ensuring that if a big wave (read: market volatility) hits one side of your boat, the other side can provide balance, and you're less likely to capsize.

Reducing Risk: By diversifying, you're spreading the risk around, making sure that no single investment or sector has the power to sink your ship. If one investment underperforms, it can be offset by others that are performing well.

Potential for Better Returns: It's not just about managing risk, though. Diversification can also help you increase your potential returns. Different assets can perform well at different times due to various factors like economic conditions, market trends, and geopolitical events. By diversifying, you're giving yourself a chance to benefit from these differing performance cycles.

Preserving Capital: Let's face it, no one likes to lose money. Diversification can help protect your hard-earned capital by not having all your eggs in one basket that could crack.

Access to More Opportunities: There's a whole world of investing opportunities out there. By diversifying, you're not limiting yourself to just one type or one region of investment. It's like having a global buffet of investment choices.

Remember though, while diversification can work wonders, it doesn't guarantee profits or protect against all losses. It's just one strategy to help manage risk and potentially increase returns. After all, investing isn't about finding a magic bullet, but about managing probabilities and making informed decisions. Diversify wisely, and let your portfolio party have a mix of all the right ingredients. Cheers to that!

2.3 Correlation and Diversification

Are you ready for some relationship advice? No, I'm not switching hats to a relationship counselor, but in investing, understanding relationships – specifically correlations – can be as crucial as understanding your significant other's food preferences. In the world of finance, 'correlation' is the statistical term for the relationship between two or more assets or investment returns.

Correlation coefficients range from -1 to +1. A correlation of +1, known as perfect positive correlation, implies that as one asset increases in value, the other will move in the same direction. Think synchronized swimmers, perfectly in tune with each other.

On the other hand, a correlation of -1, perfect negative correlation, means that as one asset increases in value, the other decreases. This is akin to a teeter-totter, when one side goes up, the other comes down.

A correlation of 0 suggests that the assets move independently of each other, like two strangers passing in the night. In other words, what one asset does has no bearing on the other.

"But how does this relate to diversification?", you may ask. Well, when diversifying your portfolio, you want to mix things up by investing in assets that are not perfectly positively correlated. A combination of assets that move independently, or even in the opposite direction to each other, can help smooth out portfolio returns. Why? Because when one asset is underperforming, the other might be on an uptrend, compensating for the losses.

Say you have a portfolio of only technology stocks. If the tech sector takes a hit, your entire portfolio feels the pain. But, let's imagine you added some healthcare stocks to the mix. If the correlation between technology and healthcare is low, the healthcare stocks might perform well even when tech is struggling. Voila, you've got yourself a cushion to soften the blow!

However, finding assets with low or negative correlations can be challenging and may change over time due to market conditions. Instead of obsessively searching for the perfect match (or mismatch, in this case), it's crucial to focus on building a diversified portfolio based on your financial goals, risk tolerance, and investment horizon. After all, in investing as in life, there's no such thing as a 'perfect' relationship. It's all about finding the right balance!

2.4 The Limits of Diversification

Diversification may seem like the superhero of the investment world, but even superheroes have their kryptonite. Understanding the limits of diversification is a bit like realizing that your favorite childhood superhero can't actually fly; it's a bit disappointing, but it's an essential part of growing up. Let's delve into the not-so-super aspects of diversification.

First, while diversification can help reduce company-specific or unsystematic risk, it doesn't help with market or systematic risk. Let's imagine you own stocks from several different sectors. If there's a significant market downturn, it'll likely affect all these sectors, regardless of how diversified you are. In other words, when a tsunami hits, all boats, no matter their size or variety, get rocked!

Second, there's such a thing as over-diversification. It's like going to a buffet and piling your plate so high that the tastes blend into each other, and you can't really enjoy anything. Similarly, if you spread your investments too thin, you could end up with average market returns at best. After all, too much of a good thing is, well, not a good thing.

Third, diversification isn't a set-it-and-forget-it strategy. It requires regular rebalancing to maintain the right asset mix as some investments may grow faster than others. If you thought diversifying meant putting your feet up and sipping on a cocktail, think again.

Lastly, diversification doesn't replace the need for doing your homework. It's not a magical wand that turns every investment into a golden goose. Researching investments, understanding your risk tolerance, and aligning your portfolio with your financial goals are all still crucial parts of the process.

In essence, diversification is an essential tool in your investment toolbox, but it's not the only one. It's like trying to build a house with just a hammer; you might be able to whack a few nails in, but without a blueprint, some quality materials, and a few other tools, you're unlikely to end up with a sturdy, let alone comfortable, house. And, let's face it, who wants to live in a wonky house? Not your investments, that's for sure!

Chapter 3: How ETFs Enhance Diversification

3.1 Broad Market Exposure

Alright, let's kick things up a notch and dive into the first subsection of chapter three, "Broad Market Exposure." This is where ETFs come on stage, strutting their stuff, and showcasing why they're the rock stars of the investment world when it comes to diversification.

Consider ETFs as your backstage pass to virtually the entire investment concert, from equities to bonds, commodities to real estate, and domestic to international markets. Broad market ETFs, like those that track a major index such as the S&P 500 or the FTSE 100, offer exposure to a large cross-section of the market in a single trade. In one fell swoop, you could potentially own a piece of hundreds or even thousands of companies. It's like owning a slice of the global economy without leaving your armchair.

Why is this a big deal? Well, it's simple. When you invest in a single stock or bond, your fortunes are tied to the success or failure of that one company or entity. But, with broad market ETFs, you're spreading the risk across a vast array of companies or bonds. If one company faces a scandal and its stock price tumbles, the impact on your overall investment will be minimal if you own shares in hundreds of other companies.

Plus, ETFs bring a smorgasbord of choices to your fingertips, from large-cap to small-cap, growth to value, and everything in between. Whether you want to rock out to the steady beats of blue-chip stocks, sway to the mellow tones of bonds, or groove to the dynamic rhythm of emerging markets, there's likely an ETF out there that can give you the broad market exposure you're looking for.

Broad market ETFs also offer an efficient way to maintain a diversified portfolio. Instead of constantly buying and selling individual stocks or bonds to keep up with market changes, you can let the ETF do the heavy lifting. The managers of the fund regularly rebalance it to align with the index it tracks.

To sum it up, broad market ETFs offer an easy, efficient way to diversify your portfolio across multiple sectors and asset classes, reducing risk and potentially increasing returns. And if that's not music to your investing ears, I don't know what is!

3.2 Sector and Industry Diversification

With a pinch of curiosity and a dollop of adventure, we're now going to take our ETF journey to the world of sector and industry diversification. Picture this: it's a sunny afternoon, you're at a picnic, and you're looking at a basket full of fruits. Sure, an apple a day keeps the doctor away, but wouldn't it be dull if that were the only fruit you ever ate? Exactly! That's where sector and industry diversification comes in.

Different sectors and industries respond differently to economic changes. Some might flourish in a robust economy, while others might hold steady when things get rough. By investing across multiple sectors and industries, you can better position your portfolio to weather different economic conditions. Here's where ETFs take the stage.

Sector and industry ETFs offer targeted exposure to specific areas of the economy, such as technology, healthcare, energy, financials, and more. Think of these as the different fruits in your basket. Having a variety of them can make your investment picnic much more enjoyable.

A technology ETF, for instance, could give you exposure to companies like Apple, Google, and Microsoft, all in one swoop. A healthcare ETF might include pharmaceutical giants, hospital corporations, and medical equipment firms. The list goes on, with ETFs for virtually every sector and industry you can think of.

Using sector and industry ETFs, you can tailor your portfolio to your expectations of which parts of the economy will perform best. If you think renewable energy is the future, there's an ETF for that. If you believe biotechnology companies are about to revolutionize healthcare, there's an ETF for that too. And, if you just can't make up your mind, why not a bit of everything?

One word of caution, though. While sector and industry ETFs can add an extra layer of diversification, they also concentrate risk within a particular area of the market. Therefore, they should be used as part of a balanced investment strategy, and not as a stand-in for broad market diversification. Like that fruit basket, you don't want only apples, no matter how shiny they look! But when used judiciously, these ETFs can be an effective tool to spice up your investment feast. Bon appétit!

3.3 International Diversification

Imagine you're at a global food festival with an empty stomach and a world of flavors at your fingertips. Would you only visit the stall from your home country, or would you venture out and sample the delicacies from around the globe? The answer seems pretty obvious, right? Well, the same logic applies to investing, and this is where international diversification comes into play.

Why limit yourself to companies based in your home country when you can tap into the potential of businesses worldwide? International diversification, in essence, involves spreading your investments across different countries and regions. And yes, you guessed it, ETFs make this as easy as pie (or should we say, as easy as international cuisine tasting?).

International ETFs offer exposure to a variety of foreign markets, from developed economies like Japan, Germany, and the United Kingdom to emerging markets such as China, India, and Brazil. Want a taste of European innovation, Asian growth, or Latin American resilience? There's an ETF for that!

Diversifying internationally can offer several benefits. First, it allows you to take advantage of growth where it happens. For instance, if the U.S. market is sluggish, but emerging markets are on fire, having some exposure to these markets could boost your returns.

Second, international diversification can help mitigate the risk associated with economic downturns in a specific country or region. Let's say your portfolio is exclusively composed of U.S. stocks, and the U.S. economy goes into a recession. In this case, your portfolio could take a serious hit. However, if you're also invested in markets that are performing well, they could potentially offset losses in your U.S. investments.

Third, different markets may not move in tandem—they could be negatively correlated or uncorrelated. For example, when it's daylight in the U.S., it's nighttime in China. If the U.S. market has a bad day (nighttime), the

Chinese market could still have a good day (their daytime). In other words, when one market zigs, the other might zag.

Now, I don't mean to make international diversification sound like a walk in the park. It comes with its own set of risks, including currency risk, geopolitical risk, and differences in regulation and market practices. But with the wide variety of international ETFs available, you can explore the world from the comfort of your investment portfolio. Ready to take your taste buds... I mean, your investments on a world tour?

3.4 Bond and Commodity ETFs

Let's get into the thick of it with Bond and Commodity ETFs, shall we? To continue with our food metaphors, think of bonds and commodities as the comforting main course and the spicy side dish of your investment feast.

Bond ETFs represent a wide spectrum of fixed-income offerings. From government bonds (tasty, reliable, but maybe a bit plain), corporate bonds (a more exciting dish, but could lead to indigestion if the company's not doing well), to municipal bonds (a local delicacy, tax-exempt in the U.S., so less taxing on your wallet), there's a veritable smorgasbord to choose from. These ETFs can offer regular income and a cushion against market volatility – like the soothing bowl of soup on a cold, uncertain day.

Bond ETFs offer a simple, affordable way to gain exposure to the bond market, which can be a bit daunting for individual investors. These funds trade on exchanges, just like their stock-based cousins, allowing investors to buy and sell them throughout the trading day at market prices. They offer diversification across a range of bonds, and the best part? You don't need to worry about when and how to buy or sell individual bonds – the fund manager does that for you. Imagine going to a restaurant and having the chef custom-make a dish for you, and all you have to do is sit back and enjoy!

Commodity ETFs, on the other hand, offer exposure to a completely different asset class – commodities. These are the things that add a dash of pizzazz to your investment portfolio. We're talking about goods like precious metals (gold, silver, platinum – the bling of your portfolio), energy (oil, natural gas), and agricultural products (corn, soybeans, and, yes, even coffee).

Commodity ETFs can act as a hedge against inflation – when the cost of goods rises, the commodities themselves typically become more valuable. These ETFs can also add a layer of diversification because commodities often have a low correlation with stocks and bonds. If stocks are taking a nosedive, commodities might be off having a party!

That said, commodities can be volatile and can sometimes turn your investment stomach. A sudden oversupply or drop in demand (remember when oil prices went negative in 2020?) Can dramatically affect their prices. However, with prudent use, these ETFs can add flavor and resilience to your portfolio.

Whether you want the steady comfort of bond ETFs or the exciting flavors of commodity ETFs, there's an investment dish out there for your portfolio. The key is a balanced investment diet!

Chapter 4: Evaluating ETFs for Your Portfolio

4.1 Understanding ETF Liquidity

Welcome, dear reader, to the maze-like world of ETF liquidity. Much like finding your way through a bustling market with a hundred different stalls, navigating ETF liquidity requires a keen sense of observation, a dash of knowledge, and a sprinkle of intuition. But don't fret, we're here to guide you through the maze, ensuring you don't get lost in the alleys of illiquid assets.

At its core, liquidity refers to the ability to quickly buy or sell an asset without causing a significant movement in its price. In the world of ETFs, liquidity is a bit of a layered cake. There's the liquidity of the ETF itself, and then there's the underlying liquidity of the assets it holds.

The first layer of the cake – the ETF liquidity – can be evaluated by looking at the ETF's trading volume. A higher trading volume indicates more active trading, making it easier for you to buy or sell the ETF without causing a significant impact on its price. It's like going to a popular market stall that always has plenty of buyers and sellers – you can quickly and easily trade what you want.

But don't let the top layer of the cake deceive you; it's the inside that counts! The second layer of liquidity – the liquidity of the ETF's underlying assets – is equally, if not more, important. If an ETF holds illiquid assets, the fund itself might struggle to create or redeem shares efficiently, which can lead to larger bid-ask spreads or even deviations from the net asset value (NAV).

The bid-ask spread – the difference between the highest price a buyer is willing to pay for an asset and the lowest price a seller is willing to accept – is a useful indicator of liquidity. A narrow bid-ask spread indicates high liquidity, while a wide bid-ask spread suggests low liquidity. It's like haggling in a market: in a bustling stall, there's little room to negotiate, but if you're the only customer, you might be able to drive a harder bargain.

Keep in mind, though, the liquidity of an ETF can change throughout the day and can vary in different market conditions. It can also be influenced by the actions of authorized participants – the big financial institutions that interact directly with the ETF issuer to create and redeem ETF shares.

In a nutshell, understanding ETF liquidity is crucial for evaluating how easily you can trade an ETF and how closely the ETF's price reflects the value of its underlying assets. It might be a complex recipe, but the taste of success when you get it right is well worth the effort!

4.2 Expense Ratios and Tracking Error

Now, what would a financial guide be without a dash of jargon? Luckily for you, dear reader, we're here to decode the mysteries of expense ratios and tracking errors - two crucial ingredients in the ETF selection broth.

Let's start with expense ratios. Simply put, an expense ratio is the cost of managing an ETF, expressed as a percentage of the fund's total assets. You can think of it as the price tag for the fund manager's expertise, the administrative costs, and other operational expenses. Now, in the investment universe, even a seemingly small difference in expense ratios can make a big impact on your returns over time. Picture it as a tiny hole in your wallet where pennies keep slipping out, and over time, you've lost a small fortune. Ouch!

A lower expense ratio is generally better, right? Well, not so fast! While keeping costs low is important, it shouldn't be the sole factor driving your ETF selection. After all, if you were buying a car, you wouldn't choose the cheapest one without considering its reliability, performance, and safety, would you?

Moving onto the next piece of the puzzle: tracking error. In the world of ETFs, many funds aim to replicate the performance of a specific index, like the S&P 500 or the FTSE 100. The tracking error measures how well the ETF follows its index. It's like a dance competition where the ETF is the contestant and the index is the dance routine. A small tracking error means the ETF is nailing the dance moves, step for step. A large tracking error, however, means the ETF is missing beats and may even be doing a completely different dance!

How can you keep an eye on tracking error? It's usually included in the ETF's fact sheet or can be calculated by comparing the fund's performance to that of its benchmark index. Keep in mind, a lower tracking error is generally preferable, indicating the fund is effectively mimicking the index.

To sum up, when evaluating ETFs for your portfolio, considering expense ratios and tracking errors is akin to checking the price and quality of a product before making a purchase. It's about finding the right balance between cost and performance, and that, dear reader, is the art and science of investing!

4.3 Assessing Underlying Holdings

In the good ol' investment world, an ETF is like a bustling, treasure-filled chest, and its underlying holdings are the precious jewels nestled inside. Each gem is an individual asset that the ETF holds, like a specific stock, bond, or commodity. Knowing what's inside your ETF treasure chest can help you make informed decisions, optimize diversification, and understand the risks and potential rewards.

When you're assessing an ETF's underlying holdings, you're essentially peering inside the chest to see the treasures it holds. Is it brimming with large-cap tech stocks? Is it a trove of emerging market bonds? Does it hold a slice of the commodities market? The answers to these questions are critical in aligning your investment strategy with the ETFs you choose.

Diversity within the treasure chest is also key. A fund that holds a wide variety of assets – like a mix of different stocks or bonds – can offer you greater diversification. It's like owning a treasure chest with a wide array of gems, rather than just a hoard of rubies. Even if one type of gem loses value, your overall treasure remains relatively stable.

Consider the weighting of the underlying holdings too. Some ETFs weight holdings equally, while others might have a larger chunk of assets tied to certain sectors or stocks. If one shiny diamond takes up half the chest, that's a significant bet on the fortunes of that single asset.

In addition, keep an eye on the fund's sector allocation. Is it heavily skewed towards technology, healthcare, or perhaps energy? Understanding sector allocation can help you align your investments with your market predictions and risk tolerance.

And finally, don't forget to look for any hidden treasures (or traps!). Some ETFs might hold derivatives, like futures or options, to help achieve their investment objectives. While these can enhance returns, they also add a layer of complexity and risk.

In the end, assessing an ETF's underlying holdings is like examining each gem in your treasure chest. It's a critical step in making sure your investments sparkle!

4.4 Evaluating the ETF Issuer

Time to pull up the curtains and meet the puppeteer behind the show, the skipper of your investment ship, the issuer of your ETFs! Yes, understanding the entity that issues, manages, and administers your ETF is as crucial as knowing what assets your ETF holds.

Why, you may ask? Picture the issuer as the head chef of a restaurant. Sure, the ingredients are vital, but who's using those ingredients to whip up your meal is just as important. A top-notch chef will not only use quality ingredients but also ensure they're mixed and cooked perfectly to serve up a delicious feast. Similarly, a reputable ETF issuer can significantly impact the success of your investment.

But, what should you consider when evaluating an ETF issuer? Well, think of it as your investment version of 'masterchef.' You want to judge the issuer's experience, size, and reputation.

A long-standing issuer who has weathered various market conditions knows how to dance in the rain and not just shine in the sun. Their experience in managing assets, navigating market volatility, and maintaining steady fund operations can be a sign of reliability and competence.

Next, the size of the issuer matters. Larger issuers often have more resources to manage their funds efficiently. They can also offer a wider variety of ETFs, giving you a more extensive menu to choose from.

Finally, take a look at the issuer's reputation. Have there been any controversies or legal issues associated with the issuer? A Google search, financial news sites, or investor forums can provide valuable insights. Think of it as reading restaurant reviews before you decide to dine there.

Choosing an ETF is not just about the fund itself. It's also about who's running the show. Before you add that ETF to your portfolio, take a moment to get to know the maestro behind the curtain.

Chapter 5: Strategic ETF Selection

5.1 Factor-Based ETFs

Pop open the hood of an ETF, and what do you find? A humming engine powered by multiple factors. These factors are the characteristics that help determine the risk/return profile of the ETF's holdings. When it comes to factor-based ETFs, these characteristics aren't simply bystanders; they're the lead actors on the stage, driving the investment strategy of the fund.

"Factor" is just another fancy financial term for traits that certain types of investments have in common. These can include size (small cap versus large cap), value (cheap versus expensive), momentum (stocks in uptrend), and quality (companies with strong fundamentals), among others.

Investing in factor-based ETFs is akin to assembling a football team. Just as a coach would strategize the team based on players' speed, agility, or strength, an investor uses factors to build a portfolio that suits their game plan.

For example, you might be a fan of David and Goliath stories and believe smaller companies have significant growth potential. In this case, you could look for ETFs focused on the 'size' factor, which will include a larger portion of small-cap stocks. Or perhaps you're more of a 'value' investor, hunting for companies trading below their intrinsic value - there are ETFs that target the 'value' factor, too.

Factor-based ETFs allow you to tilt your portfolio towards specific market characteristics that you think will perform well over time. It's like giving your portfolio a set of binoculars to zoom in on certain aspects of the market.

Of course, the choice of factors depends on your investment objectives, risk tolerance, and market outlook. Each factor has its own set of risks and rewards, and their performance can vary based on market conditions. Therefore, choosing the right factor-based ETFs requires a thorough understanding of each factor and a clear-eyed view of your investment goals.

To sum up, factor-based ETFs offer you a targeted way to invest, enabling you to align your investment strategy with specific market traits. They're the perfect tool for the strategic investor who wants a little more control over their portfolio's engine!

5.2 Thematic ETFs

Let's say you're convinced that autonomous vehicles are the future of transportation, or perhaps you believe renewable energy will power the world in the coming years. Now, wouldn't it be great if you could design your portfolio to capture these trends? Enter thematic ETFs, a type of fund that lets you do just that. Thematic ETFs are like a theme party where all the guests are united by a common interest, be it a futuristic technology, a societal trend, or an emerging sector.

These ETFs focus on capturing investment opportunities across industries, sectors, and even countries that are driven by a particular theme or trend. They might concentrate on areas like robotics, cybersecurity, healthcare innovation, environmental sustainability, or even demographic shifts like the rise of the global middle class.

Here's the deal: If you're excited about a trend and believe it will result in outperformance for certain types of companies, thematic ETFs can be your ticket to gain exposure to these opportunities. But, as Uncle Ben once told Peter Parker, "With great power comes great responsibility." In this case, the power to invest in compelling themes also brings the responsibility to understand those themes deeply.

Not all trends turn into profitable investment opportunities. Some may fizzle out sooner than expected, and others might take longer to bear fruit than you can afford to wait. Furthermore, the specific companies or sectors a thematic ETF invests in might face additional risks. A renewable energy ETF might struggle if governments cut subsidies, or a technology ETF could falter if regulators tighten rules around data privacy.

Moreover, be aware that some thematic ETFs can be quite niche, focusing on very specific or narrow trends. This could potentially lead to less diversification and higher risk.

In the end, investing in thematic ETFs is like backing your favorite contestant in a talent show. You're betting on their unique talent (the theme) to win the competition (the market). But like any talent show, there's always the risk of an unexpected outcome. Do your homework, understand the theme, and invest wisely. After all, a well-planned theme party is always more fun!

5.3 Passive vs. Active ETFs

Time for the Clash of the Titans! In the blue corner, we have passive ETFs, the low-cost, market-mimicking champions. In the red corner, we have active ETFs, the high-aiming, expert-led challengers. Who wins? Well, that's up to you to decide!

Passive ETFs are like your trusty old sedan, reliably getting you from point A to B. They aim to replicate the performance of a specific index, like the S&P 500 or the FTSE 100. These ETFs don't try to beat the market; instead, they're content to match it. They simply hold the same securities, in the same proportions, as the index they're tracking. Passive investing is built on the idea that over the long-term, the market will provide acceptable returns and trying to outperform it can be costly and risky.

Active ETFs, on the other hand, are like a sporty race car, trying to outspeed the market. They're managed by investment professionals who use their skills, experience, and research to pick and choose the securities they believe will outperform the market. This can potentially lead to higher returns, but it also comes with higher costs and risks. The 'race car' needs more maintenance, after all!

When comparing these two, consider the costs. Passive ETFs generally have lower expense ratios due to their buy-and-hold, low-turnover strategy. Active ETFs, with their constant trading and research efforts, typically come with higher fees.

Consider performance, too. Despite the best efforts of active managers, many active funds fail to outperform their benchmark index over the long term. However, a skilled active manager can take advantage of market inefficiencies and deliver superior returns in certain market conditions.

Finally, think about your investing style. If you prefer a set-it-and-forget-it approach, you might lean towards passive ETFs. But if you believe in the value of expert stock picking and don't mind paying for it, active ETFs might be more your speed.

In the end, the choice between passive and active ETFs isn't a one-size-fits-all decision. It depends on your financial goals, risk tolerance, and investment philosophy. The good news is, there's no shortage of ETFs in either camp. Whether you're team Passive or team Active, there's a perfect ETF out there for you!

5.4 Smart Beta ETFs

If you've been thinking, "Gosh, I wish there was an ETF that combines the best of both passive and active strategies," then have I got news for you! Meet Smart Beta ETFs, the ingenious brainchild of the ETF universe, which merges the low-cost appeal of passive management with the potential outperformance of active strategies. Kind of like a hybrid car, Smart Beta aims to give you the best of both worlds!

"Smart Beta" sounds like a nerdy superhero, and that's not entirely inaccurate. These ETFs aim to achieve better risk-adjusted returns than traditional market-cap-weighted indexes by using alternative index construction rules based on factors such as quality, value, volatility, dividend yield, or momentum. The goal is to exploit potential inefficiencies in the market and enhance returns or reduce risk.

If traditional market-cap-weighted ETFs are like fishing with a wide net, catching everything in a particular part of the ocean, Smart Beta ETFs are like fishing with a spear, carefully targeting specific types of fish that meet certain criteria.

For example, a Smart Beta ETF could target 'value' stocks - companies that appear underpriced compared to their intrinsic value. Another might focus on 'momentum' stocks - those with recent price trends expected to continue. Yet another might concentrate on 'low volatility' stocks - firms with a history of smaller price swings, which might be less risky.

Now, while Smart Beta ETFs sound like they've got the Midas touch, remember they're not immune to risks. They're subject to the same market, sector, and company risks as any other ETFs, and their success depends heavily on the factors they target. Just like any superhero, Smart Beta has its weaknesses, and it can underperform the broader market or its peers.

That said, if you're an investor seeking to potentially improve your portfolio's risk/return tradeoff, or you want to emphasize a specific investment factor, Smart Beta ETFs could be worth a look. It's like upgrading from your basic cable package to a premium one - you get more tailored content, but for a slightly higher cost. Smart Beta ETFs might just be the 'smart' choice for your portfolio!

Chapter 6: Incorporating ETFs into Your Portfolio

6.1 Allocation Strategies

In the world of investing, there's an age-old saying that goes, "Don't put all your eggs in one basket." This is where the magic of allocation strategies comes in. Think of it like deciding what to serve at a dinner party. You wouldn't offer just desserts, right? You'd want to provide a balanced meal, with appetizers, main courses, and yes, some sweet treats too. Similarly, an allocation strategy helps you create a balanced 'meal' for your portfolio, using ETFs as the ingredients.

Allocation strategies involve deciding how much of your portfolio to dedicate to different asset classes, sectors, geographic regions, or investment styles. ETFs, with their vast variety and specificity, make implementing these strategies a breeze.

A classic allocation strategy is the 60/40 rule, where 60% of a portfolio is invested in stocks (for growth) and 40% in bonds (for income and stability). But hey, who likes to be boxed into a classic? With the wide range of ETFs available today, you can customize your allocation to match your specific risk tolerance, financial goals, and investment horizon.

Perhaps you're a technology enthusiast who believes in the long-term potential of the tech sector. You could tilt your portfolio towards tech ETFs. Or maybe you're concerned about potential inflation. In that case, you could allocate a portion of your portfolio to commodity ETFs, which often perform well during inflationary periods.

Though, that allocation isn't a one-time event; it's an ongoing process. Over time, as market values fluctuate, your initial allocation can drift away from your desired targets. For example, if stocks have a particularly good run, you might find yourself with a higher proportion of equities than you initially planned for, altering your portfolio's risk profile.

All in all, ETFs can be the perfect tools to implement your desired allocation strategy. They provide the versatility and flexibility needed to create a diversified and balanced portfolio that aligns with your financial goals. Whether you're a meat-and-potatoes kind of investor or prefer a more exotic investment menu, ETFs have got you covered!

6.2 Rebalancing with ETFs

Picture this: you've planned a perfect road trip. Your destination is set, your playlist is prepared, and your snacks are packed. But along the way, you encounter detours, traffic jams, and maybe even a few potholes. Your original route has to be adjusted, right? Similarly, in your investment journey, your portfolio will need occasional adjustments, or rebalancing, to get back on track towards your financial destination.

Rebalancing is the process of bringing your portfolio back to its original asset allocation. It's like the guardrails on a bowling lane, gently nudging you back when you start to veer off course. And in the world of investments, ETFs can be your best rebalancing pals.

Here's how it works. Over time, as different investments perform differently, your portfolio's asset mix will likely drift from its original allocation. For example, if your equities have a banner year, they might now represent a larger chunk of your portfolio than you initially planned. By rebalancing, you'd sell some equities and buy more of other assets to get back to your original asset mix.

ETFs, with their ease of trading and broad diversification, make this process a breeze. You can easily trim overweight positions and boost underweight ones by selling or buying shares of the appropriate ETFs. Plus, with ETFs spanning every imaginable sector, asset class, and region, you can likely find one that fits your rebalancing needs.

One thing to remember is that while rebalancing is an essential part of portfolio management, it's not something you need to do daily, like brushing your teeth or feeding your pet goldfish. Too much rebalancing can lead to unnecessary trading costs and potential tax implications. Instead, consider setting rebalancing thresholds or regular check-ins – like semi-annually or annually.

In conclusion, think of rebalancing with ETFs as the tune-up your investment vehicle needs to stay in tip-top shape for the duration of your financial road trip. It's the pit stop that keeps your portfolio engine humming smoothly towards your goals!

6.3 Tax Considerations

If there's one thing as certain as death and the law of gravity, it's taxes. Even in the sphere of ETF investing, taxes are a reality that investors need to tackle. But fear not, because ETFs have a unique superpower that can help investors manage their tax implications: the "in-kind" creation and redemption process.

ETFs are structured in such a way that they can often minimize capital gains distributions. This process involves the ETF issuer and authorized participants (typically large institutional investors) swapping baskets of securities instead of cash. It's like trading baseball cards with your friends; you swap cards to get what you want without spending any money. This in-kind process prevents the fund from having to sell securities to raise cash, which would trigger a capital gain.

Though, not all ETFs are equal in the tax game. For instance, ETFs that generate a lot of income, such as bond ETFs or high-dividend stock ETFs, might lead to higher income taxes. Similarly, ETFs investing in foreign stocks might have foreign tax implications.

In the world of ETF tax efficiency, index ETFs often take the crown. Their passive strategy involves less buying and selling than their active counterparts, typically leading to fewer capital gains distributions.

One word of caution: never let the tax tail wag the investment dog. While it's important to consider tax implications, they should not be the sole driver of your investment decisions. Make sure any ETF you choose aligns first and foremost with your investment goals, risk tolerance, and time horizon.

In short, ETFs offer a tax-efficient way to access a wide array of asset classes, sectors, and investment styles. However, the tax landscape can be complex and changes regularly, so it's a good idea to consult with a tax professional to fully understand the implications for your specific situation. As the old saying goes, "It's not what you make, it's what you keep after taxes!"

6.4 Using ETFs for Income Generation

Picture this: you're lounging on a beach somewhere, sipping on a cold beverage, and you get a notification on your phone. It's your bank, telling you that you've just received a deposit. That, my friends, is the magic of income investing.

Income investing is a strategy that focuses on generating regular income from your investments, like receiving rent from a property you own. But what if you don't have a rental property and still want to get regular payouts? Well, that's where ETFs can come in and play a starring role.

ETFs can be a handy tool for income generation. There are several types of ETFs designed specifically to produce income. For instance, bond ETFs hold a collection of bonds that pay interest. This interest is distributed to the ETF shareholders, typically every month or quarter.

Or maybe you're more into stocks than bonds? No worries, there are ETFs for that! Dividend ETFs focus on companies that pay regular dividends - a portion of their profits distributed to shareholders. These ETFs collect the dividends from their underlying stocks and then distribute them to their own shareholders. It's like a dividends' merry-go-round!

And let's not forget about REIT ETFs. These funds invest in Real Estate Investment Trusts, which are companies that own and operate income-producing real estate. Reits are required to distribute at least 90% of their income to shareholders, which can make for some pretty handsome payouts.

While the lure of regular income can be appealing, it's crucial to remember that income-focused ETFs come with their own set of risks. For instance, in an increasing interest rate environment, bond ETFs might see their market value decrease. Similarly, companies might decide to cut their dividends during economic downturns.

In conclusion, if you're looking to transform your portfolio into a cash-generating machine, income-focused ETFs might just be your ticket. Whether through interest, dividends, or real estate income, these funds can add a solid income stream to your investment portfolio. Put up your feet, enjoy that beach, and let your ETFs work hard for you!

Chapter 7: Leveraging ETFs for Advanced Strategies

7.1 Leveraged and Inverse ETFs

Roll up your sleeves and fasten your seatbelts, because we're about to dive into the world of leveraged and inverse ETFs, the adrenaline junkies of the ETF universe. These are not your grandma's ETFs, and they're definitely not for the faint of heart. But, used judiciously, they can add a layer of sophistication to your investment strategy.

Leveraged ETFs aim to deliver multiples of the daily performance of the index or sector they track. For instance, a 2x leveraged ETF seeks to double the daily performance of its underlying index. If the index goes up by 1% on a given day, the leveraged ETF aims to go up by 2%. Sounds great, right? But this leverage works both ways. If the index falls by 1%, the ETF falls by 2%.

Then there are inverse ETFs, also known as "short" or "bear" ETFs. These ETFs aim to deliver the opposite of the daily performance of the index or sector they track. If the index falls by 1% on a given day, an inverse ETF aims to rise by 1%. It's like rooting for the underdog team in a game; you win when they lose.

Here's the thing, though: leveraged and inverse ETFs are complex products designed for short-term trading. They reset their leverage daily, which can lead to performance deviation from the underlying index over longer periods, especially in volatile markets. This effect, known as "compounding," can lead to unexpected results. If you're a buy-and-hold investor or someone who likes to sleep peacefully at night, these ETFs may not be for you.

In conclusion, leveraged and inverse ETFs are like the spices in your investment curry. Used appropriately, they can enhance the flavor. But too much, and they can overwhelm the dish. Use them wisely, and always within the context of a well-diversified portfolio. This is investing, not a trip to the casino!

7.2 ETFs for Hedging

Imagine you're a farmer. You plant your crops, tend to them meticulously, but at the end of the day, you're still at the mercy of the weather. Too much rain, too little rain, an unexpected frost – any of these can wipe out your hard work. What do you do? You get insurance to protect against the unforeseen. Hedging in investing works similarly, and ETFs can be your umbrella against financial storms.

Hedging is essentially insurance for your investments. It involves making an investment to reduce the risk of adverse price movements in an asset. In the context of ETFs, there are various strategies you can use to hedge your portfolio.

For instance, if you're concerned about a potential downturn in the stock market, you might consider adding an inverse ETF to your portfolio. Remember our inverse ETF friends from the last section? These ETFs aim to increase in value when their underlying index falls, potentially offsetting losses in your portfolio.

Another popular hedging strategy involves using ETFs that focus on assets traditionally considered "safe havens" during turbulent market times. This includes ETFs that invest in gold, government bonds, or certain currencies like the Japanese yen.

Alternatively, sector rotation strategies can be used for hedging. If you anticipate an economic downturn, you might use ETFs to increase your exposure to defensive sectors (like utilities or consumer staples) which are typically less affected by economic slowdowns.

Keep in mind, however, that hedging isn't free. Just like insurance, it comes with costs and can reduce your potential returns. It's also not foolproof. No hedge can fully eliminate risk, and some can even introduce new risks to your portfolio.

In summary, ETFs can serve as valuable tools for hedging your portfolio against different types of risk. But like any tool, they should be used with care and understanding. The goal isn't to eliminate risk entirely (an impossible task!), but to manage it in a way that aligns with your overall investment goals and risk tolerance.

7.3 Using ETFs for Tactical Adjustments

Ever watched a game of chess? A grandmaster doesn't just play one move at a time; they're planning several moves ahead. And sometimes, they make a tactical adjustment – they deviate from their broader strategy to seize a short-term opportunity or react to an unexpected move by their opponent. Investing can be a lot like that chess match, and ETFs can be the perfect pieces for your tactical maneuvers.

Tactical asset allocation is a dynamic investment strategy that allows you to adjust your portfolio's asset allocation to capitalize on market inefficiencies or short-term trends. ETFs, with their broad selection and easy tradability, can be the perfect vehicle for these tactical adjustments.

Imagine you see promising growth potential in the technology sector. Rather than researching and buying individual technology stocks, you could purchase a technology ETF, getting exposure to the entire sector with one transaction. If your hunch plays out and the technology sector outperforms, great! Once you feel the sector's run its course, you can easily sell the ETF and move your money elsewhere.

Similarly, ETFs can allow you to make geographic tactical adjustments. If you think emerging markets are set for a boom, you could purchase an emerging markets ETF. Or if you believe the European market will outperform, you can find an ETF for that too!

But with great power comes great responsibility. Tactical asset allocation requires a deep understanding of financial markets and careful monitoring of your investments. It's a more active investment approach and can increase your trading costs and potential tax liabilities. Not to mention, you need to be right about your market predictions, and let's be honest, none of us has a crystal ball.

In conclusion, ETFs can offer a flexible and efficient way to make tactical adjustments to your portfolio. But like a grandmaster on the chessboard, you need to make your moves carefully and strategically, always considering the broader picture of your investment goals.

7.4 ETFs in Retirement Accounts

Retirement accounts and ETFs go together like cookies and milk. With the unique advantages that both bring to the table, they can make for a delicious financial future. And don't worry, you won't have to wait until you're 65 to enjoy the benefits.

Investing in ETFs through your retirement account, like a 401(k), Traditional IRA, or Roth IRA, can be a tax-efficient way to grow your wealth. Because these accounts offer tax-deferred or even tax-free growth, they can supercharge the compounding of your ETF investments.

Imagine investing in a dividend-paying ETF within your retirement account. The dividends you earn are automatically reinvested to purchase more shares of the ETF, all without triggering a taxable event. It's like a snowball rolling downhill, getting bigger and bigger. But in this case, the snowball is your retirement savings, and there's no pesky taxman waiting at the bottom of the hill.

ETFs' versatility also means you can fine-tune your portfolio's risk level to match your retirement timeline. When you're younger and retirement is a distant speck on the horizon, you might opt for ETFs focused on growth. As you approach retirement, you could gradually shift towards more conservative ETFs, like those invested in bonds or dividend-paying stocks.

But before you start popping the champagne and dreaming about your tax-free retirement villa, remember that there are rules around these retirement accounts. Contribution limits, income restrictions, and potential penalties for early withdrawals are just a few to keep in mind.

In conclusion, while retirement might feel like a far-off future, the actions you take today can make a significant impact down the line. ETFs in your retirement account can be a powerful tool to grow your nest egg, offering tax benefits, diversification, and the flexibility to adapt to your changing needs over time. So let the cookies of ETFs and the milk of retirement accounts create a delectable recipe for your golden years!

Chapter 8: The Role of Robo-Advisors and ETFs

8.1 Understanding Robo-Advisors

Welcome to the future, where robots can clean your floors, drive your car, and even manage your investments. No, these aren't robots with lasers and a menacing laugh, but robo-advisors—digital platforms that provide automated, algorithm-driven financial planning services with little to no human supervision.

Robo-advisors make investing about as hands-off as it can get. Once you input your financial information and investment goals, these algorithms go to work, creating and managing an investment portfolio tailored to your needs. It's like having a personal trainer, but for your finances.

How do these robo-advisors decide where to put your money? Many of them use Modern Portfolio Theory, a Nobel prize-winning concept that emphasizes the benefits of diversification. The goal is to create a portfolio with the highest possible return for a given level of risk.

And this is where ETFs often come into play. Robo-advisors love ETFs, much like kids love ice cream. And why not? ETFs offer diversification, are easy to buy and sell, and come in so many varieties that there's one for nearly every slice of the market.

But before you hand over your life savings to a robot, keep in mind that robo-advisors aren't perfect. They're not great at complex financial planning, tax strategies, or understanding that you're terrified of losing money because you once lost your shirt in the Beanie Baby crash of the '90s. In other words, they lack the personal touch and holistic view that a human advisor can provide.

In short, robo-advisors can be a great tool for managing your investments, particularly if you're a beginner, have a simple financial situation, or just really like robots. With their love for ETFs, they can help you build a diversified portfolio tailored to your risk tolerance and investment goals. Just they're a tool, not a magic bullet.

8.2 How Robo-Advisors Use ETFs

Like peanut butter and jelly, robo-advisors and ETFs are a perfect match. Together, they form a potent combination that can deliver a balanced, diverse, and tailored investment portfolio with just a few clicks of a mouse. So how exactly do robo-advisors use ETFs? Grab a spoon and let's dig in.

To start with, the main ingredients in a robo-advisor's recipe are often ETFs. Due to their wide variety, low cost, and high liquidity, ETFs are ideal for crafting a well-diversified portfolio. Whether you're a conservative investor wanting more bonds or an aggressive investor seeking global stock exposure, there's an ETF to meet your needs.

Once you've set up an account with a robo-advisor, you'll be asked a series of questions to understand your financial goals, risk tolerance, and investment horizon. Think of it like a first date, but instead of asking about your favorite movies, the robo-advisor wants to know your retirement plans and what you'll do if the market tanks.

Armed with this information, the robo-advisor's algorithm will select a mix of ETFs that fits your profile. This could be a simple 60/40 split between stock and bond ETFs for a moderate investor, or a more complex mix involving sector-specific, international, or commodity ETFs.

But the robo-advisor's job doesn't end there. Like a diligent gardener, it regularly checks on your portfolio, rebalancing it back to your target allocation when necessary. And since they're trading ETFs, they can do this easily and efficiently.

Moreover, some robo-advisors use ETFs to execute more sophisticated strategies, such as tax-loss harvesting. They do this by selling an ETF that has experienced a loss and buying a similar one, allowing you to offset taxable gains while maintaining similar market exposure.

In summary, robo-advisors and ETFs are a dynamic duo in the world of investing. With robo-advisors' ability to craft and manage custom portfolios and ETFs' versatility and efficiency, they can be a powerful tool for reaching your financial goals. It's like having your personal robot butler handling your investments - just without the silver tray.

8.3 Pros and Cons of Robo-Advisor ETF Management

If you've ever tried to juggle, you'll know it's harder than it looks. Keeping track of multiple objects in the air, knowing when to catch and throw—it's a lot. Investing can feel a bit like juggling, too, especially when you're trying to manage a diversified portfolio. That's where robo-advisors come in, juggling those ETFs for you. But as with any financial service, there are pros and cons to consider.

On the pro side, robo-advisors make investing in ETFs a breeze. They handle the heavy lifting of portfolio creation, maintenance, and rebalancing. Think of it as having an autopilot for your investments, letting you sit back and enjoy the ride.

Another advantage is access to professional-grade investment strategies. Ever heard of tax-loss harvesting or automatic rebalancing? These are strategies that were once reserved for the investment elite but are now available to anyone with a robo-advisor account.

Robo-advisors also offer a cost advantage. They typically charge lower fees than traditional financial advisors. Plus, the ETFs they use often have low expense ratios, which means more of your money stays invested.

On the flip side, robo-advisors aren't perfect. While they're great at managing portfolios, they aren't so great at handling complex financial situations. If you've got a tricky tax situation or need advice on estate planning, a robo-advisor might not cut it.

Moreover, the investment options can be limited. While most robo-advisors offer a good selection of ETFs, you might not find everything you want. If you have a specific investment in mind, like a certain sector or country ETF, you might be out of luck.

Lastly, there's the issue of control. When you use a robo-advisor, you're handing over the reins to an algorithm. If you like having control over your investments and making your own decisions, this might not sit well with you.

In conclusion, robo-advisors can be a fantastic tool for managing ETFs, especially for novice investors or those with straightforward financial situations. However, they might not be the best fit for everyone. Consider your financial needs, goals, and personal preferences before deciding to go the robo-route. It's not about being a good juggler; it's about finding the best way to keep your financial balls in the air.

8.4 Evaluating Robo-Advisors

Choosing a robo-advisor is a bit like shopping for a new car. There are many models out there, each with its own set of features, costs, and performance stats. The key is finding the one that best fits your needs and budget. So let's roll up our sleeves and pop the hood on how to evaluate robo-advisors.

First, consider the cost. Robo-advisors typically charge a management fee, expressed as a percentage of your account balance. While these fees are often lower than those of human advisors, they can still eat into your returns, especially over the long term. Also, be sure to check for any hidden fees, like transfer fees or account closure fees. A penny saved is a penny earned, after all.

Next, look at the investment options. Most robo-advisors use ETFs to build their portfolios, but the range of ETFs they offer can vary. Make sure the robo-advisor you choose offers the asset classes you want to invest in, be it stocks, bonds, international markets, or even real estate.

Then, check out the robo-advisor's features and services. Does it offer automatic rebalancing? Can it handle tax-loss harvesting? What about goal-setting and retirement planning tools? You're not just buying a car; you're buying the GPS, cruise control, and heated seats too.

Another key point to consider is the minimum investment requirement. Some robo-advisors allow you to start investing with as little as $1, while others might require a hefty initial deposit. Make sure you're comfortable with the entry ticket before you hop on the robo-ride.

Finally, don't forget about customer service. Even though you're using a robo-advisor, there might be times when you want to speak to a human. Check if the robo-advisor offers customer support via phone or live chat, and see what other users say about their service.

In summary, picking the right robo-advisor is a crucial step towards successful ETF investing. It's about more than just cost; it's about finding a service that fits your investment goals, risk tolerance, and financial situation. So buckle up, start your engines, and let's hit the road to your financial future!

Chapter 9: Case Studies of Successful ETF Investing

9.1 Long-Term Diversified Portfolios

Picture the financial markets as a stormy ocean. The waves, representing short-term fluctuations, can make the waters rough and unpredictable. However, beneath the surface, the current—representing the long-term trend—continues in a steady direction. Long-term diversified portfolios are like submarines, designed to navigate these deep, steady currents, relatively unbothered by the surface storms.

Let's dissect the voyage of one such submarine, a hypothetical long-term diversified portfolio invested in ETFs. The captain, let's call her Jane, is a cautious investor eyeing a comfortable retirement in 30 years.

Jane's portfolio is the epitome of diversification, spread across a wide array of ETFs. She holds a mix of stock and bond ETFs, with stocks forming the lion's share due to her long-term horizon. She further diversifies her stock holdings across different regions, including the US, Europe, and emerging markets, through various international ETFs.

She doesn't ignore sectors either. By including sector-specific ETFs, she diversifies across industries like technology, healthcare, and utilities. She's also clued into the fact that companies of different sizes behave differently during various market conditions. She includes ETFs representing large-cap, mid-cap, and small-cap companies.

She also adds a pinch of commodity ETFs into the mix to protect against inflation and currency fluctuations, giving her portfolio a dash of spice. And she doesn't forget bond ETFs, which provide a steady stream of income and act as a cushion when stock markets take a plunge. Jane includes both corporate and government bond ETFs, from various countries and with different maturity profiles.

So how does Jane's portfolio submarine fare? Over the short term, it experiences ups and downs, impacted by market volatility, economic cycles, and global events. However, over the long term, the diversified nature of the portfolio helps mitigate these risks, smoothing out the ride.

Even during the 2028 market downturn, when tech stocks nosedived, Jane's portfolio weathered the storm. The bond and non-tech sector ETFs provided a counterbalance, preventing her portfolio from capsizing.

By the time Jane is ready to retire, her portfolio has grown significantly. Despite the occasional market storm, her long-term diversified portfolio, a veritable submarine of ETFs, has successfully navigated the financial ocean's currents. Jane can now enjoy her retirement on a sunny beach, knowing her ETF submarine has weathered the storms and arrived safely at its destination.

9.2 Tactical ETF Strategies

Suppose you consider investing a journey. In that case, a tactical ETF strategy is like a high-speed race car driven by an expert with a knack for reading the road ahead and adjusting speed and direction in real-time.

Buckle up as we take a spin in the financial fast lane with our friend, Ben. Ben is an experienced investor with a penchant for short-term market trends and anomalies. Unlike Jane from our previous story, Ben's investment horizon is shorter, and he's willing to take on more risk for potentially higher returns.

His portfolio is heavily laden with ETFs, chosen for their versatility and liquidity. But while Jane's portfolio was a set-and-forget submarine cruising steadily to its long-term destination, Ben's portfolio is a nimble race car, constantly adjusted based on the market conditions.

Ben uses sector rotation strategies to tilt his portfolio toward sectors expected to perform well in the current economic cycle. If he anticipates a booming economy, he might shift more of his portfolio into cyclical ETFs like financials and industrials. If he sees storm clouds gathering, he might switch gears to defensive sectors like utilities and consumer staples.

To execute his strategies, Ben uses a variety of ETFs, such as those tracking major sector indices, country-specific ETFs, commodity ETFs, and even inverse ETFs that increase in value when markets decline. This diverse toolkit of ETFs allows Ben to quickly adapt to changing market conditions.

Consider the Great Tech Rally of 2029. Anticipating the rally, Ben tactically increased his exposure to tech ETFs. When the rally peaked, he promptly reduced his tech holdings and moved into defensive ETFs, shielding his portfolio from the subsequent correction.

However, the road isn't always smooth for Ben. His portfolio can experience sharp turns and unexpected roadblocks, leading to significant short-term losses. Plus, the constant adjustments mean higher transaction costs. But for Ben, the potential for above-average returns makes the high-speed, bumpy ride worthwhile.

Just as every driver has a unique style, every investor has a distinct strategy. For some, a steady, diversified long-term portfolio is the way to go. For others like Ben, a tactical ETF strategy provides the thrill and potential returns they seek. Just no matter your style, always keep your eyes on the road and your hands upon the wheel.

9.3 Niche Market Exposure

The financial markets are a bit like a bustling city. There are the main streets — well-trodden paths where everyone goes. These are your broad market indices, your S&P 500s and your FTSE 100s. But then there are the hidden alleys, the nooks and crannies known only to the adventurous and curious. These are your niche markets, and with ETFs, you too can venture down these lesser-known paths.

Imagine our friend Alice. She's not content with walking down the main streets. No, she wants to explore, to discover something new and potentially rewarding. She turns to niche market ETFs to add some excitement to her portfolio.

For instance, she invests in a robotics and automation ETF, capitalizing on the growing trend of automation in various industries. When self-driving cars start making headlines, she's already ahead of the curve, thanks to an ETF focused on autonomous technology and electric vehicles.

Then there's the esports ETF in her portfolio. Yes, that's right, professional video gaming. As esports gain mainstream recognition and attract massive audiences, Alice's portfolio rides along on the digital coattails of this emerging sector.

She doesn't stop at the border either. A country-specific ETF lets her tap into the economic growth of an emerging market without the need for individual stock picking. When the emerging market takes off, Alice's portfolio soars too.

But Alice's adventure isn't always rosy. Niche market ETFs often involve higher risks and can be more volatile. For example, a sudden shift in technology could impact her robotics ETF, or a political crisis might shake her emerging market ETF. They are also subject to the idiosyncrasies of the specific sector or region they represent.

Yet, the potential for high returns lures Alice down these intriguing alleyways of the financial markets. By using ETFs, she can navigate these niche markets with relative ease, adding a dash of adventure and the potential for high rewards to her investment journey.

The next time you find yourself wandering down the main streets of the financial city, remember there's a whole labyrinth of interesting, lesser-explored paths you can venture down. And with ETFs, you don't even need a map!

9.4 Active Management with ETFs

A symphony is only as good as its conductor. Similarly, an actively managed portfolio is only as good as its manager. It's a dance of timing, precision, and strategy, with ETFs playing the instruments of diversification and tactical investing.

Allow me to introduce you to Carlos, our maestro in the orchestra of active investing. He believes in the power of superior asset selection and market timing to generate returns above a benchmark index. His baton? A wide array of ETFs, expertly selected and combined to create his unique investing symphony.

Carlos doesn't buy the whole "market efficiency" argument. He believes some securities are undervalued or overpriced at any given time. Unlike the passive investing crowd who stick to the rhythm of the market, Carlos tries to beat the tune.

He uses sector-specific ETFs to overweight sectors he expects to outperform, based on his analysis of macroeconomic indicators, industry trends, and market sentiment. He also uses inverse and leveraged ETFs to profit from anticipated market declines or to amplify returns in a bull market.

In addition, he might use bond ETFs with different maturity profiles to position his portfolio in anticipation of interest rate changes. If he foresees a rate hike, he might switch to short-term bond ETFs to minimize price depreciation.

But let's make no mistake: this style of investing isn't for the faint-hearted. It requires a profound understanding of the market dynamics, constant monitoring, and timely decision-making. It's like conducting an orchestra, where each instrument (ETF) must play in harmony with the others to create a beautiful symphony (profitable portfolio).

And just like conducting, there's no guarantee of success. The markets are full of uncertainty, and even the best analysis can't predict all outcomes. Active management also often involves higher transaction costs, which can eat into the portfolio's returns.

Yet, for Carlos, the potential to outperform the market makes it worth the effort. He keeps fine-tuning his ETF selection, timing his trades, and conducting his investing symphony. In the grand orchestra of the financial market,

Carlos is a maestro, skillfully directing his ETFs to play the sweet melody of above-market returns.

Chapter 10: Emerging Trends in ETF Investing

10.1 The Rise of ESG ETFs

Picture a three-legged stool. Each leg represents a component of ESG: Environmental, Social, and Governance. Alone, each leg is weak, but together, they form a stable platform that's becoming increasingly attractive in the world of investing. ESG ETFs, once a niche player, are now stepping into the limelight, and it's about time we gave them the standing ovation they deserve.

Let's be clear: ESG is not about chaining yourself to a tree or boycotting corporations. It's about investing in companies that have sustainable business practices, promote social justice, and have robust corporate governance structures. It's about aligning your investment dollars with your values, and ETFs are making this easier than ever.

ESG ETFs track indices composed of companies meeting specific ESG criteria. For example, an environmental ETF might invest in companies with low carbon footprints or those actively engaged in renewable energy. Social ETFs might focus on firms promoting diversity and fair labor practices. Governance ETFs might lean towards companies with strong shareholder rights and transparent executive compensation policies.

Just five years ago, ESG ETFs were the quiet kid in the back of the class. But they've been hitting the books, hard. In fact, the popularity of ESG ETFs has exploded, with assets under management growing at a phenomenal rate.

And why not? ESG ETFs offer investors a simple and cost-effective way to invest sustainably.

But as any seasoned investor knows, every investment has its risks. ESG ETFs are no different. There can be a lack of standardization in ESG ratings, which means one firm's "green" might be another's "light green." Furthermore, some critics argue that ESG ETFs can have higher expense ratios than traditional ETFs, potentially eating into your returns.

Still, in a world increasingly conscious of climate change, social justice, and corporate accountability, ESG ETFs are emerging as the new rockstars of the investment arena. And just like any rockstar worth their salt, they're shaking things up, transforming the landscape, and making investors worldwide sit up and listen. Investing no longer has to be a choice between your wallet and your conscience. With ESG ETFs, you can have your green cake and eat it too!

10.2 Cryptocurrency and Blockchain ETFs

Think of cryptocurrencies and blockchain technology as the bad boy rockstars of the financial world. They're new, they're rebellious, and they're causing quite the disruption. For investors with a taste for innovation and a stomach for volatility, ETFs focusing on cryptocurrencies and blockchain might be your backstage pass to the show.

Cryptocurrency ETFs essentially aim to track the performance of a single cryptocurrency or a basket of different cryptocurrencies. This way, investors can gain exposure to this dynamic and rapidly evolving asset class without the hassle of managing digital wallets or grappling with blockchain technology. In other words, you get to rock out at the concert without having to deal with the rowdy crowd.

Then there are blockchain ETFs, which invest in companies that are developing or heavily using blockchain technology. Blockchain is the foundation on which cryptocurrencies are built, but its potential use cases extend far beyond that, including supply chain management, healthcare, and finance. By investing in a blockchain ETF, you're buying a ticket to a performance that's about more than just the headline act.

Let's not forget, though, that this is a rock concert, not a classical music recital. Cryptocurrencies are notoriously volatile, subject to dramatic price swings that can make a rollercoaster ride seem like a gentle stroll in the park. The regulatory environment around cryptocurrencies is also in flux and can impact their value significantly.

As for blockchain, while its potential is immense, it's still early days. Many companies included in blockchain ETFs are in the experimental stage, meaning the risk of failure is high.

In short, cryptocurrency and blockchain ETFs aren't for the faint-hearted. But for those with a taste for disruption and a tolerance for risk, they offer an exciting opportunity to invest in technologies that could reshape our future. They're the wild drum solos and electrifying guitar riffs in the symphony of ETF investing. Just be sure you're ready to rock and roll with the punches!

10.3 Innovations in ETF Structures

In the grand financial fashion show, Exchange Traded Funds have always been the ready-to-wear collection: accessible, diverse, and ready for the taking. But who said they can't be haute couture? Welcome to the runway of ETF structures, where innovation and creativity meet practical investing.

First up is the model of Active Non-Transparent ETFs (ants). You see, traditional ETFs are as transparent as freshly cleaned glass windows, revealing all their holdings on a daily basis. But ants, they play hard to get. They offer the best of both worlds: the active management of mutual funds and the trading flexibility of ETFs, but without revealing their holdings daily. A little mystery can be attractive, can't it?

Another head-turner on our runway is the concept of thematic ETFs. Thematic ETFs are not just about sectors or indexes; they're about narratives. They focus on powerful macro-level trends and future-forward sectors like clean energy, artificial intelligence, or even space travel! Yes, that's right. Space. The final frontier could be part of your portfolio. Beam me up, Scotty!

But what's a fashion show without a few unusual pieces that catch the eye? Enter Buffer ETFs. These ETFs are designed to limit your losses if the market goes down, but there's a catch: they also cap your gains if the market goes up. A bit like wearing a bold, avant-garde outfit, it might not be for everyone, but it certainly stands out in a crowd.

However, these innovative structures come with their own set of caveats. Non-transparent ETFs might not appeal to those who value transparency in their investment choices. Thematic ETFs might involve more risk because they're often concentrated in a narrow area. Buffer ETFs, while providing some downside protection, can limit your upside in a booming market.

In the fashion-forward world of ETFs, there's never a dull moment. New structures and models are constantly in the works, each with their unique spin on investing. Just remember to match your ETF style with your financial goals and risk tolerance. After all, in the world of ETF haute couture, one size does not fit all!

10.4 The Future of ETFs

Welcome to the time machine! Seatbelts fastened? Great, because we're about to zoom forward to explore the future landscape of ETF investing. As we approach this brave new world, we'll find that it's not just about the assets we invest in, but also how we invest in them.

In the realm of portfolio construction, we'll likely see a growing shift towards ETF managed portfolios. Think of these as a ready-made meal; an entire portfolio composed entirely of ETFs and managed by professionals. These portfolios can cover a wide range of strategies, from income generation to capital appreciation, offering a one-stop-shop for investors looking to diversify.

As technology continues to evolve at warp speed, the way we trade ETFs will also change. Could we see ETF trading via blockchain technology? It's a real possibility. The transparency and security offered by blockchain make it an attractive option, not to mention the speed and efficiency of settling trades on a decentralized ledger.

And what about the assets themselves? As global economic trends evolve, so too will the ETFs that track them. We could see an increase in ETFs that focus on emerging markets, particularly in Africa and Southeast Asia, as these regions continue to grow and develop. As climate change continues to dominate global conversation, we're likely to see an expansion in ETFs focusing on renewable energy and sustainable practices.

While it's exciting to ponder the future of ETFs, remember that with every forward leap comes new challenges and risks. Regulatory changes, market volatility, technological glitches, and shifts in global economies can all impact the ETF landscape. But that's all part of the thrill of investing, isn't it?

As we step out of our time machine and back into the present, let's not forget the most crucial thing about the future of ETFs: they will continue to evolve, adapt, and offer investors a wide array of choices to suit their individual needs, risk tolerance, and investment goals. Because, ultimately, that's what ETFs are all about: putting the power of investing in your hands. Back to the future, indeed!

Chapter 11: Common Pitfalls and How to Avoid Them

11.1 Overdiversification

Picture this: you're at a buffet with an endless variety of foods. There's pizza, sushi, pasta, tacos, curry, cakes, salads, and more. You want to taste everything, so you heap your plate with a little bit of all the dishes. But after a few bites, you realize that you can't really taste anything because your taste buds are overwhelmed. Plus, your plate looks like a chaotic mess. That, my friend, is the culinary equivalent of overdiversification in investing.

Overdiversification, or diworsification as some affectionately call it, happens when an investor's portfolio is spread too thinly across too many investments. It's like trying to follow every rainbow in the hopes of finding a pot of gold at the end of each one. In reality, all you end up doing is running around getting wet.

With ETFs, it's easy to fall into the overdiversification trap. After all, one of the major benefits of ETFs is the ability to access a wide variety of asset classes, sectors, and geographical regions. But just because you can eat all the dishes at the buffet, doesn't mean you should.

Having a slice of every possible investment pie may seem like a sound strategy for risk reduction. In reality, though, it can dilute potential returns and make it harder to monitor your portfolio. After all, keeping track of a hundred different ETFs can be about as easy as herding cats.

On top of that, having too many similar investments might result in redundant exposure. This is like going to a buffet and taking five different kinds of mashed potatoes. Sure, they all have a slightly different flavor, but at the end of the day, they're all just mashed potatoes.

The solution? Focus on achieving balance rather than collecting investments like they're going out of style. Carefully consider each ETF's role in your portfolio, and remember: sometimes, less really is more. Now, go forth and buffet like a pro!

11.2 Ignoring Costs and Taxes

Remember when you were a kid, and you'd carefully count out your pennies to buy that shiny toy from the store? Now, imagine getting to the checkout only to discover that the actual price is much higher because of additional costs. Nobody warned you about those, right? Well, in the world of ETFs, those hidden extra costs are real and can give you quite a financial pinch if you ignore them.

Costs associated with ETFs can creep up on you like that crafty raccoon that keeps raiding your garbage bins at night. They are sneaky, relentless, and can make a real mess of your investment returns.

Consider expense ratios. This annual fee, which covers the fund's operational costs, may seem tiny — perhaps 0.2% or even less. But let's not be deceived by its small size. Much like the fleas on your pet dog, these little suckers can add up and become a significant nuisance. Over time, even a seemingly small expense ratio can eat into your investment returns.

Then there's the bid-ask spread, the difference between what buyers are willing to pay for an ETF (the bid) and what sellers are asking for it (the ask). Ignore this, and you might end up overpaying for your ETF or underselling it when you're ready to part ways.

But wait, there's more! Let's not forget about brokerage fees. Each time you buy or sell an ETF, your broker might charge you a commission. Some brokers offer commission-free ETFs, but as with all free things in life, it's essential to read the fine print.

Now, onto the taxman. Much like death and that darn raccoon, taxes are unavoidable. Capital gains, dividend income, and foreign tax withholdings are all subject to taxation, and the rules can be as complex as quantum physics on a bad day.

Bottom line: costs and taxes matter. They're like the gravitational pull on your ETF rocket, subtly affecting its trajectory. Ignoring them won't make them go away. Keep your eyes wide open, and make sure to factor in all costs and taxes when considering your potential net returns. Your future self will thank you.

11.3 Misunderstanding the Purpose of an ETF

Picture this scenario: You've bought a brand new, high-end hammer because you heard it's the best tool in the market. But instead of using it to pound nails, you try to use it to slice bread. We all know how that's going to turn out, right? The bread is in crumbs and your high-end hammer is smeared with butter and jam.

This, in essence, is what happens when you misunderstand the purpose of an ETF. Each ETF is designed with a specific purpose in mind, be it tracking a particular index, focusing on a certain sector, offering exposure to a specific geographical region, or providing a unique investment strategy like Smart Beta or thematic investing.

ETFs are not one-size-fits-all. Trying to use an emerging markets ETF when you need a steady income is akin to using a hammer to slice bread. It just won't work. Or imagine going on a safari hoping to see polar bears. You'd be pretty disappointed, wouldn't you? That's exactly what you'd feel when you invest in an ETF expecting performance that it isn't designed to deliver.

To prevent this kind of heartbreak and confusion, you need to understand the purpose of each ETF in your portfolio. What index does it track? What assets does it hold? What strategy does it follow? Understanding the ETF's purpose will help ensure that it fits into your overall investment strategy, meets your financial goals, and is in line with your risk tolerance.

As investors, we must remember that no single ETF is a magic wand that will solve all our investment needs. Each one is a tool, designed for a specific task. Before adding any ETF to your portfolio, take the time to understand its purpose. Because unlike that high-end hammer, you can't just wipe off the butter and jam and start over.

11.4 Chasing Performance

Imagine this: your friend got a pet cheetah, and now it's the fastest thing in town. Seeing this, you decide to get a cheetah too, hoping it'll give you the same thrill. However, by the time you get yours, it turns out to be a lazy couch potato who loves binge-watching wildlife documentaries. The moral? Chasing the fastest isn't always the best idea. The same principle applies to ETF investing.

Chasing performance refers to the practice of selecting ETFs based on their past performance. It's a strategy as tempting as a chocolate cake at midnight. After all, it seems to make sense - if an ETF performed well in the past, it should continue to do so, right? Wrong. This is like expecting your newly-adopted cheetah to win races because its sibling did.

The financial markets are a complex beast. Just like our lazy cheetah friend, they don't care about past performance. An ETF that outperformed its peers last year, last month, or even yesterday, isn't guaranteed to continue that streak. Countless factors, including market conditions, economic changes, and even news events, can influence an ETF's performance.

Moreover, chasing performance can lead to an unnecessary increase in trading activity. This means more brokerage fees and possibly more taxes, both of which can gnaw at your returns like termites on a wooden fence.

Investing in ETFs isn't about choosing the fastest cheetah. It's about choosing the right blend of ETFs that can help you achieve your financial goals. Don't be swayed by the seductive song of past performance. Instead, focus on your investment objectives, risk tolerance, and time horizon. The race is long, and it's only with yourself. Choose your cheetahs wisely, and maybe keep a couch handy, just in case!

Chapter 12: Conclusion: Crafting Your ETF Investment Strategy

12.1 Reviewing Key Takeaways

So here we are, at the end of our journey through the intricate labyrinth of ETFs. Let's take a moment to dust off our boots, pat ourselves on the back, and review some of the key nuggets of wisdom we've picked up along the way.

We've learned that ETFs, or Exchange-Traded Funds, are investment vehicles that track indices, sectors, commodities, or a collection of assets. These financial chameleons are traded on an exchange, just like individual stocks, and offer a balance between diversification and liquidity that could give even the most zen of monks a run for their money.

We've learned about the history of ETFs, from their humble beginnings in the 1990s to their booming popularity today. We've seen how they've evolved, diversifying into myriad types and structures, each with its own set of benefits and risks.

We've discovered the magic of diversification and the role of ETFs in achieving it. We've understood that ETFs are not a one-stop solution for diversification, but rather, a means to gain broad market exposure, sector-specific concentration, international reach, and even access to bonds and commodities.

We've also dived into the nitty-gritty of evaluating ETFs. We've tackled topics like liquidity, expense ratios, tracking errors, underlying holdings, and even the reputation of the ETF issuer. We've emphasized that while selecting ETFs, one must always wear their detective hats and look beyond the glossy brochure.

Next, we've navigated through the vast ocean of ETF selection strategies, exploring territories like factor-based, thematic, passive, active, and smart beta ETFs. We've recognized that every ETF has its unique charm and purpose, much like the unique characters in a blockbuster movie.

We've learned how to incorporate ETFs into our portfolio, balancing allocations, using them for income generation, and even considering tax implications. We've also delved into advanced ETF strategies, including leveraging, hedging, tactical adjustments, and their use in retirement accounts.

Finally, we've studied the pitfalls that every ETF investor should avoid. Overdiversification, ignoring costs and taxes, misunderstanding the ETF's purpose, and chasing performance - we've discussed these perils and how to avoid them.

In essence, we've painted a holistic picture of the world of ETFs, one that's not just vibrant with opportunities but also speckled with challenges. Every stroke of knowledge adds depth to this masterpiece, enabling you to craft your own successful ETF investment strategy. Now, ready to venture forth into the world of ETF investing? Let's go!

12.2 Creating Your ETF Action Plan

Okay, folks, this is it - the big moment! We've learned the alphabet, now it's time to write that poem. In other words, we're moving from understanding ETFs to creating your personalized ETF action plan.

Put on your best thinking hat and let's dive right in. First up, define your investment goals. Are you saving for a house? Planning for your retirement? Or building an emergency fund? It's like deciding on your vacation destination before you start packing.

Next, evaluate your risk tolerance. This is your financial comfort zone, the range within which you can stomach the ups and downs of the market without losing sleep. If you're someone who gets queasy at the first sign of turbulence, you might want to stick to more conservative, lower-risk ETFs. If, however, you're the thrill-seeking, skydiving type, higher-risk ETFs might be right up your alley.

Then, determine your investment horizon. How long can you afford to keep your money invested? If you need it next year for a down payment on a house, you'll have a different strategy than if you're saving for a retirement that's 30 years away.

With these three pieces in place, you can now select the ETFs that align with your goals, risk tolerance, and investment horizon. Remember the multitude of ETF types we discussed? Here's where you choose from them. Consider the sector, region, index, or strategy that each ETF targets, and pick those that complement your overall investment strategy.

Allocate your assets among these chosen ETFs. Keep in mind the principles of diversification and your own risk tolerance. Don't put all your eggs in one basket, no matter how shiny the basket looks.

78

Once your portfolio is set up, monitor it regularly. Keep an eye on the market trends, the performance of your ETFs, and any changes in your personal financial situation.

Lastly, be patient and disciplined. Investing is a marathon, not a sprint. Resist the urge to react to short-term market fluctuations and stick to your plan.

And there you have it, your very own ETF action plan! It's like a treasure map, guiding you towards your financial goals. Hoist the sails, set your course, and embark on your ETF investing journey!

12.3 Staying Informed and Adapting Your Strategy

Alright, mate, let's tackle this next piece like a boomerang that always comes back to its original spot: staying informed and adapting your strategy. You see, the world of ETF investing isn't static. It's as dynamic as a kangaroo on a trampoline. Things change, and if you're not ready to roll with the punches, you might find yourself outpaced quicker than a koala up a gum tree.

Staying informed isn't just about reading financial news or following market trends (though those things are important). It's about a continuous learning process. Yes, much like your granny's never-ending knitting project, there's always more to add on to your investment knowledge.

Keep an eye on changes in the ETF landscape. New types of ETFs are introduced regularly. They could be based on evolving sectors, emerging markets, or innovative strategies. Who knows? Maybe there's an ETF out there for kangaroo-based businesses in the works!

Similarly, ETF regulations can change. Keep yourself updated on these changes and understand how they could impact your investments. If there's a change in how ETFs are taxed or how they can be traded, you'll want to know about it quicker than a dingo snatching your lunch.

Most importantly, keep track of your own financial situation. If you've recently changed jobs, had a baby, bought a house, or gone through any other significant life change, your financial goals, risk tolerance, and investment horizon could all be affected. This might warrant a review and possible adjustment of your ETF investment strategy.

An ETF investment strategy isn't carved in stone. It's more like a sketch on a drawing board, ready to be tweaked as necessary. Keep those erasers handy, and don't be afraid to redraw your investment plans as needed. After all, the only constant in life is change, right?

12.4 Encouraging Continued Learning

As we wrap up our ETF adventure, let's not forget the importance of the journey itself - continued learning. You've made it through the thickets and emerged on the other side with a robust understanding of ETFs and how to incorporate them into your investment strategy. But don't put your explorer hat away just yet, because the world of investing is a vast jungle of never-ending discoveries.

ETF investing, much like gourmet cooking or perfecting the art of origami, requires continuous education. You've got to keep learning about the latest investment trends, new regulatory policies, the emergence of innovative ETF products, and much more. If you're not evolving with the market, you might as well be a woolly mammoth stuck in the last ice age.

Take advantage of the plethora of resources available today. Webinars, online courses, podcasts, industry reports, and investment blogs - all these are your guides on the path of continued education. Some might say it's like having your personal financial Yoda, only without the green skin and peculiar sentence structure.

Participate in investing communities, too. They provide a platform for you to learn from others' experiences and mistakes. Someone else's misstep can be your stepping stone.

Always question your knowledge and assumptions. Just when you think you know all there is to know about an investment subject, you discover a new perspective that changes everything. Be open to new ideas and willing to challenge your own beliefs. After all, growth happens outside your comfort zone.

Learning is a never-ending process. It's like trying to fill a bottomless cup, the more you pour into it, the more it can hold. Keep pouring in knowledge and wisdom about ETF investing. Your future self, sitting on a beach sipping a fancy drink with a tiny umbrella, will thank you for it.

www.ingramcontent.com/pod-product-compliance
Lightning Source LLC
Chambersburg PA
CBHW072340290526
45794CB00002B/949